THE ONION
FLOWER

THE ONION FLOWER

AND OTHER CONTEMPORARY, ABSTRACT AND EXPERIMENTAL POEMS

Michael A. J. Sardo

Writers Club Press
San Jose New York Lincoln Shanghai

The Onion Flower
And other Contemporary, Abstract and Experimental Poems

Writers Club Press
an imprint of iUniverse.com, Inc.

For information address:
iUniverse.com, Inc.
5220 S 16th, Ste. 200
Lincoln, NE 68512
www.iuniverse.com

ISBN: 0-595-19584-9

Printed in the United States of America

Books by Michael A. J. Sardo

A Cycle of Poems in Experimentation 1953 (out of print)

A Cycle of Poems in Experimentation Continued

A Collection of Contemporary and Abstract Poetry

Little Italia and Other Contemporary Poems

A Tribute To New York City in the 1950's

"She sang Like an Angel" and Other Contemporary Poems:
A Tribute to My African American Friends

The Onion Flower and Other Contemporary, Abstract
and Experimental Poems

Prologue

In writing this small collection of Abstract, Contemporary and Experimental Poems, I have blended my conscious with my unconscious thoughts. How I achieved some of my ideas and impressions to write these verses was to allow my mind to take me on a field trip or journey into a relaxed part of my soul that wanted all-out, uninhibited freedom to write.

I would like to share this with my readers: I approached this book differently by writing down on paper the titles of each poem and then creating the rest of the poem or the body, from that point on. I'm not an early riser, I like working at night mostly. Working on the edge of my bed is the most comfortable position for me. Slowly, in the A.M. hours, I look at what I have written the night before for reexamination and revision. Writing everything in longhand is my method; typing is not my thing. My knowledge of computers and keyboards is nil. That's about as old-fashioned as I want to be. Writing poetry to me is fun. In my own way I feel I have something to say in this particular art form. I encourage young writers everywhere I go to keep writing.

Introduction

Abstract painters mix colors of different hues to create a panorama of visual sensations. Sometimes a doctrine emerges on their canvasses. A doctrine of emotions, passions and feelings are birthed on the work surfaces. The way the paint is applied makes up the marked difference between mediocrity and genius.

Poets that dare to be different and venture into this vast wasteland are very often misunderstood and their work is branded as hybrid junk. Over and over again words and silent sounds emerge from a verse that seemed obscure to the naked eye. The rules of form are given up for adoption; correctness is left to the writers that seek monetary and material recognition. This volume of Abstract and Experimental poetry breaks the polyphonic barrier.

The dragon slayer is mobile and optional. The critic cannot compare jazz with popular songs. Neither can a critic compare contemporary, abstract, experimental poetry with the magnificent poetry of William Shakespeare, Lord Byron, Shelley or Keats. There is a place for abstract experimental poetry in the Twenty-First Century and especially for the destiny shapers involved in it.

Thoughts on Abstract Poetry

Contemporary, abstract poetry is an art form that gratifies,
and establishes in modern thinking an image of life.
Because of the complexities of 21st Century living
this medium of expression is sometimes experimental in
nature and may often be mistaken as primitive and bewildering.
Not so I say dear fellow poets, keep writing this way.

Libraries

Libraries in the U. S. which own Michael A. J. Sardo's *A Cycle of Poems in Experimentation (1953) and A Cycle of Poems in Experimentation Continued (2000)* and Other Collections*

Glendale Central Library, Glendale, California
Occidental Library, Occidental, California
Sheean Library, Illinois Wesleyan University, Bloomington , Illinois
University of Illinois, Urbana, Illinois
Burrage Library, Olivet, Michigan
William R. Perkins Library, Duke University, Durham, North Carolina*
New Mexico State University Library, Las Cruces, New Mexico
Kent State University Library, Kent, Ohio
Edward W. King Library, Miami University, Oxford, Ohio
John Carter Brown Library, Brown University, Providence, Rhode Island
Harry Ransom Humanities Library, University of Texas, Austin, Texas
Earl Gregg Swem Library, College of William and Mary, Williamsburg, Virginia
Colonel Robert H. Morse Library, Beloit College, Beloit, Wisconsin
New York Public Library, Humanities and Social Sciences Library, New York, N.Y.

*Includes the following:
A Collection of Contemporary and Abstract Poetry
A Tribute to New York City in the 1950's
Little Italia and Other Contemporary Poems

Contents

Acknowledgment

I wish to acknowledge Tina Roberts who was kind and patient in typing this manuscript. Most of all, I appreciate the fact that she never questioned why I was writing certain verses and never made any comments or changes in the script. Abstract, contemporary and experimental poetry sometimes seems like it has a mind of it's own

PASSING THROUGH

Every existence has a sequel of variables.
Does someone have the ability to verbalize
Slotted schedules and misfits amount very little
Burning sands passing through the shingles
Multiply sorrow in clear cut glass daylight
Problem solvers passing through. Break up time.
Against brick walls. Brick walls terminating
Political follies. Revelations of post prophets.
Vocalizing in umbrella pain. Overdrawn accounts
Dolor often brings her black lilies
Daylight clashes shuttled bright victories
Passing through every keyhole of time
Paridiso is on its way. Blowing hard
Against the black snow passing through
the eye of the camel. Back up. Stop passing through
Timpani skins get up tight and thunder.
Passing through vibrant sonics petering rain
Out in the principles strong habitation outlawing
The heavy oil spills of Imperialism in Tropical Isles
Every moment caught in limbo
Passing through

OPEN WINDOW

Somewhere in the subconscious. Dumping out impressions
In unison with awe inspiring thumping edges
Cloning, cloning: beasts and mortals
Running, jumping astounding aliens and gremlins too
Slicing a piece of yesterday
Looking through the hierarchy of insolent paradoxes
He stands naked not running after lost inhibitions
Affirming his stance in cyberspace
His Mongoloidian dreamscapes. Nourish his trauma
Unencumbered by off-white empty canvasses
The Tincture of Iodine tastes sweet to him
In an empty soda bottle. He telescopes the open window
The flute, tambourine and recorder pour out a cautious resonance
Through the open window of ocean floors
The pilot light burns the unholy incense
Through the pits of Gehenna, The fires burn savagely
In an unorthodox game. Winner takes all
Find a lost horizon: through a magnifying glass
By popular vote the satyr has it.

Michael A. J. Sardo

Mid-course Circuit Breaker

Heavy, clobbery shoes keep the electric
out: Parliament disengages. Without overtime
the course the Barrister follows. Coinciding
with spring breaks. Highlighting anguish
ridden, dirty streets. Polluted drinking
vapid aqua. Running, jumping, stumbling
Mid-course not mid-life. Procuring
a way of dying undaunted. Crystals gleaming
in the murky atmosphere. Around
and the semi-circle chanting is ominously conceived. Laura
Belle primps up for the sordid encounter.
The oxidizer is the agent. A little on point
Vaseline and contact is made clean in. Sparks:
Fly from the generator common ground
insulation from the voltage refractor.
Press the pound key. Keep the circuit alive now and
forever more. Politely negating the offense.

Glazed Apples and Tangerine Skins

The color red. Called Jelly Apple on a stick
Dorothy's shoes are bright on the way to Oz
Brilliant forays in white and yellow daisies
Glazed apples! Glazed apples!
Too nice looking to eat. Entrepreneur, connoisseur.
Open the brown bag. And look in. See Me Baker
Strips of Tangerine skins rolled in honey. A sugar treatment
Squeeze some more free Tangerine skin. Unblemished.
Strike a match: look into the little explosions
As your head pounds in an eardrum beat. Smell
the Tangerine skins.

Michael A. J. Sardo

Botanical Garden Outpouring

Green shoots reverse their growing pains
Garden fragrances are atomized
like an earthen scent from a greenhouse ward
vines, roots, seedling and plants find their way
across the Eskimo's garden spot. The Operating Room
every conceivable doxology finds honor in botanicals
Even the sinister man-eating cannibal plants can swallow
a dog if necessary. Call it quits. Botany professors still
study in their glass houses. Complexities of
being a thinking, alive plant. Never trying to repossess
themselves. Don't be a glutton.
Pour out a vat full of chlorophyll microbes.

The Onion Flower

Thin like paper. Outside an ugly parchment
The white makes you growl and tear
Somewhere in the heat of an oven broiler
Without any sugar. Who savored the taste
Onion glower perishable unnoticed in fireless heat
cows eat and spit out sour milk of goats
Onion flower bouquet of rotten stench
On the way to the crematorium filled with octaves
taste the thin skin slices on the vegetable treat
Onion flower take a wine bath in a pan of liquid slush
Fry in an oily reservoir and feed from the empty trough
can you ever leave the human skin without a scent
Blooming onion flower of little significance
Onion Flower! Botanical freak. Belong somewhere!
   Onion Flower! Figment of the mind of shadows
      Onion Flower! Smelly flake of odor
         Take a bath onion flower
           Now is your hour

Michael A. J. Sardo

A Season of Suppression

Now it's over
What was it before
Before it was over: It spewed out
Memories, emotions, Fantasies, Nightmares
Opaque colors, gray clouds, hurt feet, aching bones
All these years and you finally tore open the containers
Desires, dreams, pleasures, joys, loves lost
Friends, enemies, liars, villains, more
healing balm, cleansing salve, ointment
Gone astray, always rejections
Walking Alone, misjudged
Mistrusted, Judged now
Put away the times
Locked in a glass key

Non-existent Fragrance

Dissolution at no smell of pretty roses
The mask of destroyed senses
plays havoc. Song in your brain
The noise in your head you hear
From the 30's and 40's the radiators sing
Songs of steam heat and whistling valves
Some lived in cold water flats
All they could smell was produce wood boxes burning
Produce wood boxes from the pushcarts downstairs
Everything smelled; but not of cooking
Imagination void of fragrance
Starving; the smell of perking coffee in your mind
And fried potatoes in the black iron skillets
No smell, no fragrances, not even boiling water
making a troubled nail soup. Was an existence
then and now. Sniff all you can.
Single-minded odorless world

Michael A. J. Sardo

Pleasing the Inner Ear

Who cares about the Federal Reserve when your ear makes you dizzy
Your nausea hangs on a little way
Flat on the floor, still the room spins
Some feelings: each vying for your attention, hurting feels nice
Depression is a way of life. Some can't live without it.
To be unhappy makes you happy. Happy, happy turmoil
All sounds are audible even to the deaf
Parade up and down Main Street U.S.A. with a nice migraine
Why fight over a stinkin' nickel
He said choke on a pickle
Fashions, styles, and detachments wail out loud
Crying sands overwhelm the terrain of the crowd
Humid nights suggest: cry in the rain
And who's to blame. Psychic pain.
Semi Circular sensations. Serum spilling out in blunt rage
Judgment passed out-puts you in a cage
Can't you feel something. Like the alien's log entry
Martian you look different. A man from gentry

Discord Even Among the Martians

Where is that place called Utopia?
Somewhere on the Red Planet. No. No.
Even the Selenites disagreed
Discord produced the inter galactical frenzy
So popular among humans. Habitating off on planet Earth
Garble and high strung chatter among the apes
Fusion of energy ovum producing crystalline sperm
There's order in the interplanetary Tribunal Council
Peace in space, peace in the Universe. Peace
The opiate of human energizers. Nowhere around
Timeless cooperation among the visionaries of space
Nocturnal blasts through the open doors of the mind
Telepathy under control of intelligent beings
Sweet taste of warm atmosphere blanketed all over

Michael A. J. Sardo

Shooting Pain in the Head

Noise from the clattering El on Brooklyn shores
Monstrosities even more
Was the electric drill probing a skull
Or was it a bullet penetrating the head
Repressed feeling chained in a cell of the mind
Compartments of pain in the tenement brain
Inferiority and rejection ate away the will
Branding iron. Fiery hot. Coming through the right side
Lamenting on-looker. Couldn't do a thing
To ease the pain. And the loss of gain
A hot narrow spike penetrating the day
Through the telescope. See cells in the ray
Terrorizing the whole and lobo
Without a purpose and no gain in jobo
Add a ringworm to the itching mess
Nails pricking out of purple roses make for mental stress

Be Deceived by Their Lies

Political strategist rumble phonetically
Disburse hatred and tension ironically
Format discs magnify the sounds of primary
Color. In front of mirror reflections of.
Who's who in rusting dungeons. Piercing
Hair shirts cry out from the lies. Of
the vanquishing conniver silver tongued
falsely humble Rumpelstiltskin run away. Always
talking like a never ending endless loop tape
Capable of any disenchanting flagrancy. Blooming
crab trees and olive branches. Slippery
Eels, mud sucking inhabitors of the
Lying, deceiving, glowing, ugly, vicious dream
factory. Of Holocaust memories and blood
Baths of purging dictators. Deceivers hustling
for another deceitful earth tremor

Michael A. J. Sardo

East Faces West

Endless Timeless Relentless
Come to grips with past experiences
Your burning eyes see very little decline
Defeated in the forties era
Only to rise up and bring forth great things
Starting with European-Asiatic relationships
From the shores of the beautiful Pacific
Musical genius, Technological gyrations exploding
Causing spoiled competition to shape up
The Chans and Lees waste very little
From the unpopular war of the sixties
To the university unrest and more
And then the ugly Foreigner made love
To the once enemy Islander: She could have
Planted bombs: tamed by love. Continents
Apart. Kissed and made. Only to forget napalm
West learned Eastern ways
East latched on to Western displays
No difference either way. Only if you look
For the unfair, prejudicial interplay.

Elegy of a Bashful Buffoon

Histrionics, Annals of maelstrom
Negating in a windfall of hungry humor
Pain hidden in comedian's face
Trying so hard to put away the disgrace
Anxious for nothing. Positive of everything
Cry and cry. More crying and injury added to insult
What wasted talent. A product of mental abuse
From the first summer day of the put down movement
Be funny and please their faces
No matter what personal pain and hurt you endure
Be the jovial leg stretcher who
Pulls his face from right to left always
Crying it hurts. Who would believe the
Comedian. It hurts. It hurts. Now Y. Now Y.

Michael A. J. Sardo

Sweet Scent of Innocence

Pliable aphrodisiacs hidden in a storm
They play and laugh with impish faces
Their colors like the hues of crayons
Or colored Easter eggs in a basket of green
Artificial grass. Chocolate bunnies and
Yellow marshmallow chicks. Never
the real chicks of the 50's. Never
the cruelty of the Shoppe on Madison Avenue
Singing the nursery rhymes of the make
believe. Without fear. With total
Trust. Playing happy games among
themselves. They may even have called
it. No inhibitions in this time of innocence
Playing, laughing and singing in their
little strawberry jumpers. Kittens
puppies and the beautiful white dove
smelling only the smell of the pollen from
all kinds of garden flowers. Playing the
bright sunlight open air theatre

Counteraction Among Friends

Who's a friend
Who's an enemy
Even among friends
Even among enemies
Even in the Industrial Revolution
Even in the Renaissance of Thought
Even in the Age of Miracles of Medicine
Even in the Age of Genetics
Of DNA's of clones and more clones
    Even in Test Tube of Life
    and Test Tube lies
    In the space- time continuum
    and the Potter's Field Graves
    Even in the Barb Wire confines
    Even among the beasts and animals of human civilization
Disagreement in the slave market
Disagreement in the prejudicial, judgmental market
    Balls, Jacks, Rubber bands and Dominos
    Friends of paper clips, staples and carbon paper
    Friends of friendships of lost dreams
    Thoughts and imaginations
    Even on St Valentine's Day

Michael A. J. Sardo

The Magnitude of the Monster

In theory and essence it's smaller than a microbe
Larger than a cell
Raging and warring is this virus
More destructive than the Bubonic plague
Fiercer than a nuclear blast
Overshadowing the future and the past
The perfect fool chambered in his requiem
Even microscopic life was frantic
Judgment was final
Ask the monster why
In his silence he refused to lie
His domain galaxies and star filled light systems
With no reigns and control the monster ran wild

Making a Place for Different Ones

Make a place for Different Ones!
>In your county
>In your city
>In your state
>In your country
>In your village

Make a place for Different Ones!
>White race
>Black race
>Yellow race

Make a place for Different Ones!
>Black man
>Red man
>Oriental man
>Brown man
>Yellow man
>White man

Make a place for Different Ones!
>Humanity
>Frailty
>God's image
>Private
>Peculiar
>Fleshly
>Finite
>Mortal

Make a place for Different Ones! Only Human

Recharge Your Battery
—the Adversity is Over

You play the Honest Game
You play the Fair Game
You play the Compassionate Game

Your energy level is expended
Your cheek is turned the other way
Your high level of decency has run its course

Time to rest
Time to re-energize
Time to minimize. Seemed important at the time
Time to re-enter and start the climb

The old man lost his racial hate
The old lady lost her racial fear
Ironic time-piece. It's over now.
When you depend on that different flesh tone

Your Past Has Been Blotted Out

What goes in, is one matter. What goes out another
Refreshing cool breezes. Push out past promises
Past mistakes, grotesque flash backs
don't seem to care or worry. In explosions of
Lights of different complexions and magnitudes
The screen replenishes with alien looks and friendly
Travelers. Rejection, loneliness and
Single mindedness cooperate to bring glamour
Back to stay. Old fashion kerosene lamps
Burn their wicks out to nothing. The
Little purple capsule under the inhale glass
of water coincides with passion for conversation
The stinging heat arrows in the subconscious
are gone. And wonder of amnesia is here
to stay. And the troubled spot finds the blotter

Michael A. J. Sardo

Boomerang

Flagrant steel shining in the moon-light rays
A hope of returning   Back from
Point A to point B end a quandary of mis-
chief. Exonerated by the chief Judge High
and Mighty. Australian friends learned it's
Use in the day of the volcanic eruptions amid all
the ashes, the gray ashes, the ashes of heat
The empty ash urns, the cover up ashes of the prophet
Job. Someone even tried the accurate flying weapon
against a friendless enemy.

Direct Line

Exercising great caution
Deceiver of no one
Going for simply happiness
At all cost making verses
Relating to a valentine
Allowing the cautious Raven in
Lingering from the after effect
loving all he could have of life
And then none
Nope just the lusty, dust left behind
Politely say no way man
on top of the acid situation
Eaves made of platinum

Little cottage in the Bronx N.Y.

Michael A. J. Sardo

Ornament of Elegance Rediscovered

As I walked the soot ridden street. And
I saw the remarkable. And the many more things.
Mr. Dixie played songs on the dirty
Old, worn looking; tarnished green saxophone.
As his nimble fingers, played with the keys.
Melody so smooth outweighed his look of poverty
Only his talent outspoken from the little
bar. Filled with smoke and beer smells.
Crying encore, encore. You sound like
Yard bird, was heard from the ornament elegant
ageless. Revitalizing the past in a now neutral situation
Ferreting out the ornament

Celestial Spaces

Flying in great spaces succumbing to her graces
At Heaven's gate, we seldom ate
the curtain came down. No sight of the clown
Restitution was made, flounder in facade
Crystals turned vapors of light. Turning
The night into a great fright. Flamboyant
Telescopes saw the Milky Way. A heavy
Price to pay. Heavenly bodies crying
Out Celestial places. Your trip in atmospheric
spaces

Michael A. J. Sardo

Figure of Speech

A word you didn't mean to say
Because you did very little thinking
Composing wasn't your thing
Deception was the old lady's thing
Ecologically to the point
Fatoora in Sicilian was her name
Geographically in consistent were her ways
Humor, morbid humor: Fatoora screamed
I want some semblance of peace
Journeying from brown bag to brown bag
Killing with your tongue hurts
Longing for love sometimes remote
Motivating even the slow-poke
Nothing but a slip of the little member
Owl's say very little. Even in graveyards
Please. When you think of saying it
Quivering at the thought of commitment
Results forth coming in the marathon
Suspicious, even of the bird songs
Triple tongue the mouth piece
Universal time of untamed winds
Victories lost and won over words
Witness the glowing dark victory
Xylophones responding to mallets of control
Your time has come: Now!
Zambia place of unrest

The Definition of Hunger

A hurting gut even in America
Soup kitchens
and even super-market dumpsters
Hunger running a muck
In the Third World and:
even U.S.A. cities
Begging for coins to eat scraps
Cut away the rotten and eat the good
A spoiled child spitting out necessities
To maintain the life of a pot bellied
weak little tyke. Younger than she looks
Look that's a bloat of famine!
Emerging, published. Not a day of fasting
A day of going hungry. They look like victims
of the Nazi Concentration Camps. A Holocaust
of humiliation at nothing to eat

Michael A. J. Sardo

Outraged

Temperance freaked out in turmoil
Whose tendrils engage violent paroxysms
Lunacy disengaged in energized hostility
Who's afraid of Opal Wintwert? Smilin'
Jack the Cracker Jack. Full of degrees
Can't seem to get a good paying job
Too creative for his own skin color
Empty, hollow cadaver died a vegetable
Not a mollusk
Just an outraged representative of mankind

Soliloquy

Salty pretzel sticks
Ultra thin morsels even to hicks
Where's my speech to say
In the folio edition: on it's way
Everyone speaks to himself in a mirror
Adjusting something of a vanity scissor
Hamlet spoke more than one
His anger and pain was no fun
Over and Over he spoke the speech
In the Danish land he tried to preach

Michael A. J. Sardo

Love Broke the Barrier

Love minces no words
Love doesn't care
Love finds a right place
Love doesn't have a home
      Love cares
      Love dares
      Love understands
      Love maintains equality
            Love is music
            Love is open pages
            Love is tender words
            Love is probing
      In time
      It takes time
      Even in it's prime
      A spotless timepiece
Magnitude of sensitivity
In keeping with equality
Formulating a plan
A gentle plan
of action. Trying to make the mark
An open fortress in the glime
            Love Cool!
            Love Straight!
            Love Gone!
            Love-breaker
No color   No difference   Ageless   No Gender   Atom

Who's Afraid of a Skeptic

Virginia Wolff
Nan Ringle
Oscar Symthe
Ironic vibration consort to an honor system deflated
A cracker eater
A day laborer
A gold-digger lady
A substitute for the real thing when there's no coke
A gambler volunteering his wares
A coxie's army nightmare
A swish with delicate Flair'
A speechless campaigning undernourished lobbyist. Ouch!
A little bird chirping
Godzilla doing his thing
An actor, an understudy
A Peace Officer
Justice of the Peace
A brilliant black lawyer
A swish unable to make the grade at the Bar
Simple people
Timid people
Withdrawn people
Timorous, demure folk
dunderpate friend
The harlequin
For whose sake are you crying, Mr. Synchronism?

Oliver was a Cat

Magnificent Tiger of the Alley. On Broadway.
White Chestnut, white paws, corpulent feline friend
Knew his name. When called. Oliver! Oliver!
No degree from an Ivy League school
More smarts than a well trained...........Poodle Cool
        A kitty who found a bedspread
        And loved Mr. Egghead
        A friend who liked shortbread
        Oliver killed a copperhead
Oliver the cat was great
Oliver you dared not dominate
Tough as nails. Hard to frustrate
Oliver was a great housemate
Oliver had teeth like a piranha
And hated the smell of toasted marijuana
He didn't come from a junction called Bwana
Oliver fell in love with an Africana cat

Anger as the Day Goes By

Slip-shod but nice
Unrelenting kindness showing in every nook
Trying delicately to please
Rejection at every turn of the screw
A power play. Why not walk away.
Hate him because he's gay
Looking in your steamer trunk
Lift the lid and let out all the junk
Indignation could be called righteous
When there is cause for alarm
looking through the amber colored lenses
Watching the day-by-day injustices go by
You want to scream out-loud
Everything gets to you. As you see the crowd

Michael A. J. Sardo

Resistance to the Norm

Strike the hammerhead against the concrete
Watch for the spark
Not that many sparks
City blocks and City sidewalks
As old as the hills
Antiquated funnels of emotions
Normality what is your surname
Resounding Answers. Resisting the straight regime
Block and tackle products of a mindset
Normalcy what is your antidote?
The last page with the footnote

Narrowness Found It's

Cover story
Anchor
Blue Light
Narrowness Found It's
way between two vehicles
between two options
scarlet thread
opium den
O'Leary's Trip
Narrowness Found It's
formulated criteria
place in society
in the Everglades
Narrowness found It's
unction to be deceased
perimeter to be boxed
way to be found
Not Guilty! Not Guilty!
Narrowness Found It's
way out
fall out
down-spout
strikeout
worn out
brown out
down and out
trucked out
fluked out

Michael A. J. Sardo

A Jar of Empty Relish

Scrape the bowels of the glass enclosure
Empty, Empty, Empty. Void of all particles
and taste buds cry out for a little tang.
If you could be a magician
or miracle worker and talk to the jar.
Fill up. Just a little more. Desiring
a microwave feast of dog and bun
just a little treat to placate the morsel
desire. Promise never again let it ever run
out. Empty jar. Give birth to a little spoonful.
Just so I don't have to leave the comforts
of home T.V. and Fast-food commercials.
Fill just a little and enough empty
glass blown jar. You're the star of this night
empty relish jar

Concerning the Natural World

Come into my home Star Trek. My living room.
Different kinds of peoples from different planets
Who's the Captain of this Star-Ship?

Concerning the Natural World!!
Hard to escape. Your responsibilities now!
Earning a living is prime time
Food on the table might mean over time
Children need clothes and things. Just like Queens and Kings
Moms and Dads buy the nice things
Three kids. Each one spoiled in his own way
Working to make things A-OK
And now concerning those great teens
Who want nothing but designer jeans

Blameless Time Keeper

X-rays, gamma rays, opulent rays
lost in time and within the Bell Jar
He slew the vapor dragonfly
Promised to keep time to limitless nine
Emissions polluting the air a crime
Without polar intervention. Atomic clocks. Work
temporary onslaught of generous slime.
Protracted outcome viral fever urn
Temporary relief stare in a last good turn
concocted from nothing to make something.
Plagiarized every timeless contract
Adam stayed awhile acting dumber with every breath
East winds at the lost and found. Claimed Eve.
Mother of lies
Garnet flavored Easter rolls
Quick and easy. Lease another car.
Your friend from P.R. Smiled
Wants Jamaican? Companions and Friends
Must be the rum.

Nonessential Facts

Who has time to criticize and not circumcise
take time and fraternize
run in the Italian Sun
hurting feet want to make you run
aside from the fire and the heat
The lesson you've learned is never retreat
Prolific writers and their flagrant ideas,
sometimes cause the malice makers to accept fears
Facts climb up the stairs of the unnecessary
Climatically the blows from the wind speak only the necessary

Michael A. J. Sardo

The Flip Side of the Coin

Got kicked in the groin
Spat on like dirt on the underfoot
Nothing he did to desire and deserve this treatment
They were proud, arrogant. And in gray
Their teachers never taught them to pray
They couldn't stay
    inhuman acts of cruelty was their play
The liberators came that day
    Even innocent children had a say
Who's face is on this coin?
The man you kicked in the groin
Explanations,
Explanations and more
    and even more explanations
    the pilot light went out
    incorruptible judge won this bout
    and every other bout
Came the year forty-eight
The guerillas carried all their hate this time
    Relentless, never stop hunting
    Remembering the torture racks
        Even little children did
    Guilty! Hangman. Ready
    Guilty! Pass the time
Flame thrower, burn the rats
    Watch them run
By all means them's rats. Diseased rats

Escapist

Out of an altered innovation
The eye of escape spoke emendation
A vertical black box with the semblance of a grim coffin
The magical scientific explanation was the Answer
Mandrake the Magician solved the top hat mystery
Houdini, blew the mind of gullible society
Often time. Upstarts pushed their way in
Flammable party antics found the route home
Party hats. Horn blower. Even Roman Candles
Was the tale of woe and market value
Rock bottom platitudes of winning the game
A poet's shirt cost big bucks. Now
Was finely ruffled and elegant then.
Practitioner of sorcery you know the black arts,
And how to eject from the company of props

Michael A. J. Sardo

Preventing the Murder of Julius

A thrust of cold brute metal in the bowel, almost.
Could have prevented the hideous act. And did
What would the Empire have done. If?
Without "Friends Romans Countrymen" crying out
There were no ears for listening to Anthony
And no soothsayer bewailing the Ides
Across the coliseum. Roaring animals silenced
A field of rain put out the jealous fire. Among
The Senators, Landowners, Poets and Politicians
All this. And much more of a calm before
Caesar, Roman Emperor of the World
Your murder didn't take place. The volcanoes
Were silenced. And history was altered. And
Shakespeare penned nothing. Look at this coin. And
Examine both sides before it's given name
The name of prevented occurrences never reenacted

Analgesico

The International Fashion Preview passed
Over a hard shell insensitivity to feelings
                    to emotions
                    to tenderness
A stammering pain overlooked the Calico Cat
Even a Calico Cat could feel rejection
Post trauma expressions of lurid outlooks. Invaders
Ingrained from early childhood flashes
Cold—dark empty cavity
Void of feelings of potency
Robotian images from a laboratory
Like needing a new tuning fork. Right now.
And being a self-appointed unknown deity
Motionless gears, cogs, pulleys and wheels
With an inability to feel pain
Vulgar smelling coke fumes dissolving in the rain
And the ostentatious fraternity of the partisan ended
Go with the wind, feel no pain
Receive no tactical gain. The preview is over
The solicitude of retaliation spoke of a foul stench

Michael A. J. Sardo

Cinema Astratto

Fifty million fruitcakes lined up in a row
Playing with stars of the platinum screen
Gays, Lesbians, Self-righteous, and unsavory characters
All passed in review, in sinister drag attire
Polluting the minds of the judges
Even the dogs sniffed their way into the dress rehearsal
In plain view and uninhibited in their motives
Local correspondents made their way back to Main Street
Where Cinema Astratto was conceived

Pizza in a Hurry

Called Pie
Inlaid spiced mixture
Crust covered
Not an American Tragedy
Having no pity, Tummy tum
An experiment in imbibition
Ascendancy in art baking

Even the fast foods esteem the pie
From Italy a far flung cry
Red wine from a chalice
Lips large and belonging to Alice

Pizza in a hurry
Can't wait Mr. Murray

Michael A. J. Sardo

When Does It End?

Consequently never and forever
For information call Dylan Ever
It never does, and never will
Looking for political perfection?
Social Utopian cornerstones
Excessively devoted to submission
He maintained priggish expectance forever
It terminated in the Sarcophagus of Transparency

Thwart the Enemy

Through unrequited love
Through selfless generosity. Unable to define
And through your love and prayers. The outcome benign
Your enemy hates tenderness
Without knowing why. Alienated from society
Very little time for propriety
Unfavorable decision maker follow your plan
Grand Street. Grander Market Place
No black sheets or virgin whit coffin antics
Americano show your presence on the vine
Reverse the scope of the treatment
Pollute a little, vacillate the single joint
Protest, little discrepancy is noiseless.
The twilight zone pleads vacancy

Michael A. J. Sardo

Rancid Peanuts

They lay all over the streets of the city
Not rancid peanuts
Rancid humans
Homeless, hungry, dirty, cold, shivering
Smelly, consumptive, sweaty, untouchables
The stench of cheap wine
Tobacco smelling stained threads
Overlooking the river traffic on the lonely street
The old white-haired gentleman gasping for oxygen
Washed his bearded face with dry gin
No foreigner to starvation and shame
The ambulance came finally. After a time
And took what was once a part of the human species
Caring was the lost spiritual gift in this time span
The crew of the dying earthlings, concerned
Noted, the insignificant little cellophane bag
A prize possession falling from his shirt pocket
Some Rancid Peanuts again
A tale of cold unconcerned citizens
In a city of Rancid Peanuts and Rancid Humans

The Audacity of Them

Refusing to walk the cobblestone path
Rejecting talent because of unwanted judgments
Because of the dark lenses they wore. Clouded
Crystal wafers of light. Rejecting because
The difference was evident. Time will tell.
Meanwhile don't care. Deformed at birth
Wanting acceptance. Then no tolerance
Wandering from task to taskmaster. No
Different than a foreigner in a new domain
Procrastinator refusing to be fair. Decision
In favor of the familiar face. Refusing
To acknowledge ability because of preconceived judgment
Refusing to make an attempt to understand the difference
Reorganize and revamp the regrouped mindset

Michael A. J. Sardo

Phantoms Disappear

In the forests of the mind
In the glass of Mirror Lake
In polluted streams and rivers
In heavy unbreathable atmospheres
In the ozoneless air bubbles
In pages of unwritten legacies
In harbored prejudicial judgments
In gloomy, quiet library tomes
In polite make-believe embellishments
In faces of refusers of change
In pompous strong-willed stubborns
In gray haired staunch conformists
In money hungry caring pretenders
In a cloud of terrestrial smoke
In the faint glimmer of hope
In an evaporated liquid sustenance
In the tentacles of unrequited love

PHANTOMS DISAPPEAR

Regret Decisions Made

Like crustations hanging around the inner most recesses
Flashing back echoes of lost memories
Like the tree that was chopped down venomously
Lightning flashes on a March night. Thunder storms in April
Pointed questions refusing to be answered discommodiously
How void the life of the decision maker
In a clouded unsettled mind tempered in deceit
Looking through a stinking stitch in time
A scandalous offshoot of withered foliage
Show and Tell confounding a dwarfed ego
Concentric hollows terminating the empty man
Echoes of a train-ride never completed
Getting off at the wrong station, looking back
Living the rest of the years in secluded glamorous loneliness
They were made. Later on regretted, healing time where are you?

Michael A. J. Sardo

Religious Writings

Moral present events colliding with destiny
With sudden violent double-mindedness
Documents filled with ornamentation and legalism
Acquittals, exonerations and absolutions to the letter of the law
Documents defining chastisement and castigation
Papers dealing with the All-Powerful- One
Religious writings filled with Guardian Angel Love
Deity challenged by evil molester
And more documentation of succuba and spectral images
The writings go on and on. Full of Theology; Revelation:
Demonology, Orthodoxy, Religious Truth, Holiness and
Heterodoxy. Pious religious writings

Is It Free?

Emancipation from what? Provision never made.
Recompense in cowardly thoughtlessness
Desiring the question to be answered by the proletariat
Honor bound with very little superciliousness
No it's not!
Low cost problem solver. No you're not!
Try some poet. He knows the commentary
A bushel of silver quarters resembling an unveiling
Disco dancing, a term of evasiveness
Denver calling New York for a fix
No it's not!
Stop looking for short cuts. Newness is here
Florence found favor from Francesca's fantasies
For men and women of loneliness uncertainty was reality
The pendulum swung inquiringly for the last time
No it's not!
No it's not!
No it's not!
What's free?

Michael A. J. Sardo

The Inoculation

a sharp needle makes a valley in your skin
almost like a ripple in water
how could a needle be so clean and sharp
cost a lot of dough even with medicare
you drill for this, and that
what you get is some serum in the brain
are you a gladiator with shoes of skin
popularity makes for peer pressure now and then
don't get inoculated with a tainted probe
or the drilling you do in your body is wasted
wait five minutes for friendly hallucinations
inoculations may be good for people eaters
and sink-hole swamp for light-headed bikers
don't care how you feel now or in an hour
the inoculation fever will get you
in due time you'll be like the rest of them
since the party is over
let's go see Jon and Lizzy

Money Matters

Product of environment
Rat trap environment
Never had $ and c's
Read current events
Like blasting caps
Jackhammer pecking
Save. What's that
A way of eating chicken fat
Don't read labels
Just sock it away
On everyday pay
It all didn't pay off after all.

Poetic Justice

When the scales tip to one side
And the lady with the wreath around her head has no control
The laws have finally been transmuted
Rebellion among the populace is the side effect
Like blemished fruit
Truth has accurately justified virtue
A marriage of golf ball and caddies come to zero

The Drama

No gain, No pain, refrain. The play
With a cast of actors gay, in gray attire
Dumb struck. Dumb stroke. Not of genius
Curtain call. Parts, 5 minutes 'till curtain call.
Night after night even Shakespeare was bored
Live actors, who never acted before
Neighborhood workshops. Working
Thespian outlaws trying to make the mark
Talent used and never wasted. Unadulterated
Scripts, character analysis in due time
Outside the walls of the Globe. He wrote
Master Creator of Drama. He wrote as the
Bard. He was the Bard. He said the play's
Thing. And a flurry of horns not sounding like
Trumpets, or coronets blare mercilessly.
Life's panorama of montages passed. For
The ages and generations to come. A
Plague consuming all the island was the drama

Michael A. J. Sardo

Unobtrusive Mr. Yates

Mr. Yates
Loves Gates
    Humble Mr. Yates.
    Simple Mr. Yates.
        Loves iron gates
        Palm trees, freight rates
            Walking with Mr. Yates
            Policy-making Mr. Yates
                There is a talented man Mr. Yates
                His name Mr. Yates or Mr. Gates
                    Talented, gently and kind
                    Is the quiet Mr. Gates
                        Pin drop quiet
                        No flair for egoism
                            Winning is the name of the race
                            Mr. Yates or Mr. Gates

Got Any Candy

Patent leather shoes
Bobby Green hats
Candy man where are you. See you Sammy
In a tree that grew up in Brooklyn, Mr. Davis Junior.
Find ten men and then you'll find the juror
Cover stories all about them magazines. That,
The boys wearing seersucker shirts read out loud
All about. Or hand over the candy Man. Hey, got any candy?
See the young vampire wearing the black pique knit shirt.
Or the Indiana Smith wearing the expedition hat
Here's the candy man in the canoe with the stone bucket hat
Sammy he's got lots of candy.

Michael A. J. Sardo

Souvenir Shop

Products of fractured relationships. Never growing up
Incidental music coming from the little shop.
Souvenirs come alive at the crack of dawn
Shop of broken home souvenirs coming alive
Ardent seekers pretending to be buyers
Don't judge the gator by his looks
Crossbreed him with an anaconda
And there will be enough skin to cut a thousand shoes
The largest inventory of tapestry bags in Morocco and Bombay
Find the shop it's around the corner.
Filled with delights of horror

Chinese Fortune Cookies

Tasty cakes accentuated by prophetic documents
Piled high in stacks of tens. Shells of air
The Chinese philosophy fills the atmosphere
Conclusion to the sumptuous meal. Oriental.
Why the spaghetti questioned the uninformed
Because the thin noodle was born in China
And much more wisdom from behind the Great Wall
Among the inner circle it was more than a cookie
More than a sweet conclusion. Timing, title and pride
Honor to the Tang Dynasty of hero's
In the elite circle of non-pretentious intelligentsia
The Chinese fortune cookie opening the mind
For the printing presses and the fatal gunpowder
All born within the Great Wall

Michael A. J. Sardo

Baroque Music

Sounds set in a dark era, electrify a society
A shroud of gray images caught up in sorcery
Vibrating strings a tribute to phonetics
A music stimulating the mind intensely unintentional
Protected by the puritanical clergy
Was it another DaVinci creation or a mathematical resonance
No discord just a theme of dulcet notation
A music so significant you were transported to the churches
Far from drawing rooms of pomp and splendor
A meaningful configuration of synchronized music
Flourishing in the Papal inner circle. The open door
To the great musical geniuses to come
In all their grandeur. Adorned in greatness to come
And the organ pipes cried out to be heard

Salad Bars at Fast Food Restaurants

Try to find one
Far and few among the Fast-Foodacholics
Anymore a thing of the past
An experiment which failed
Never got off to a good start

Salad Bars Otherwise

The small mid-western town
Eatery extravaganza
Sunday noon and after
Every off-base glutton was there
Gorging like famished vultures
Breakfast, lunch and supper devouring all
Gormandizing the food bar. A challenge
Making a pig of oneself. Epicurean human
Running from the Church Sunday PM
Droves of gorgers practicing little temperance
Exploding outward in their Sunday best
Running the race of waist measurement
Why the doldrums?
Substitution instead of enchantment
A dissertation on home-life
Every ethnic and racial representation came
And there were the Oriental Salad Bars too

Michael A. J. Sardo

Turn Down

Eradication, the rejection syndrome
The trauma of getting no for an answer
Mind games the same one they played in Rome
The Gladiators and the crowds at the Coliseum
Thumbs down
The intention was evil. Costumes hideous
Absence of motive. Cataclysmic dividends
Thumbs down. Bent upon a mean design
A harsh decision. Rejection formula. Outpost Sahara
Oasis in the desert, a trip after the cube
Without dextrose. The obvious one-way street
A bottomed out failure. Oblivious intersection
A feeling, an emotion, the big renunciation out of wedlock.
Armor piercing innocence fully receiving the rebuff

The Invention of the Chimera

Organic artificial brain tissue innovation!
Diversified genetic miniature colony. The insinuation!
Finding safety in a cup of hibernation. The creation!
The intern examined the chart with fear. The energizer!!
Trepidation caused the alarmist to Bello
Forlorned treasure of blameless anti-bliss. The margin!
Reproduction without tensile strength. Problem-solving coordinates!
Playmates in a sea of microbes. The monumental Goof-off!
Polarizing the whole Zoo of the mind. The invention!
Into one brainchild
Into one conception
Into one apprehension
Into one supposition
Into one thematic curiosity
Investigating the whole yolk for interrogation
Why Chimera?
To find the castles in the atmosphere

Michael A. J. Sardo

Dream the Dream

When instability stands in your way
Dream the dream
When indecision haunts your daily presence
Dream the dream
When meaningless jibber-jabber stalks your stygian past
Dream the dream
When judicial skeptics form opinions of you
Dream the dream
When good intenders pursue your disaster course
Dream the dream
When envious so-called friends invade your promised land
Dream the dream
When cacophonous factory noises invade your head
Dream the dream
When pleasing sweet sounds of symphonic music caress your soul
Create the dream
When resplendent effulgent light rays invade your spirit
Work the dream

Intensify Your Creativity

At any given moment drive hard your precious gifts
Whether writing, painting or daydreaming. Keep
It up. Keep going. Continue walking. Add strumming
Adjusting your creative portfolio daily. Using good
Sense. Paper from legal pads of different
Colors. Intensify your efforts at eliminating regret
Let melancholy and merriment entwine in the inner-circle
Of friends and loved ones. Exonerate global
Differences by writing a treatise on love.
Procure the advice of someone of a different color,
A different import, or even a different design
Intensify, fortify, amplify, petrify, nullify. Simply sanctify
Creativity belongs where it ratifies, every single bar-fly.

Samples of Wisdom

The little red ant works feverishly to engineer her mound
Birds and geese and things fly soon to the sunny South
That was a lie. A big fat lie. From the very beginning
Close the casket while there's time.
Buy the very best all the time
Tinkering toys teach garden closets how to tell time
Tin soldiers play with bottles of olive oil
Fat-free aerosols deplete the ozone layer
And flies and things are generally bewildering
Ding dong, ping-pong! Wind up the timepiece
If you get hungry in less than an hour CRY WOLF
Vipers eat anchovies out of the cans, as fast as cats

Words Can Make You or Break You

Prolific sentences bind guidelines to empty pages
A slip of the glib tongue, misuse can pluck out verbal attacks
Simple sentences, compound sentences, complex sentences
With subjects, predicates, and objects diagramming,
structures can create havoc in the precise humanoid
A slip, the right kind of slip. A palpable slip. Can
Herd a small flock of sad stories. With stammering
Lips and a countenance of enthusiasm. Ego tears down ego.
Make mention of turgid, euphonious words and you
Have an immoral breakdown, and no voice in libretto
Loved one minute, hated the next. Formless, speckled
Serpent camouflaged in the absence of a situation

Michael A. J. Sardo

The Empty House

A temple lacking consecration
A place of worship, cold as a morgue
A residence without living beings
A bungalow lacking cheer
A bricks and mortar painful structure
An igloo of indifferent time limits
Columbined with missing faces
A conscienceless penitent sybarite
A pleasure-seeker feeling no compassion
A money-hungry executive
A concert hall without an orchestra
A blackguard wanting flattery

Dry Toast

It popped out of the broiler. 10 minutes ago
Or some hungry bird had it with a worm
Dry toast under foot crunched by daylight
Implementing. The first OK of left over "K" rations
In your knapsack dry toast. Left-over from
Breakfast, lunch or supper. A simple
Non-prescription for acid heartburn. Without Dr. Lee's
Hand in written hieroglyphic platitudes
Dry toast a substitute for sawdust in a
Butcher Shoppe in the village. In the
Shoppe of Horrors choking out your
Life's last breath. Oasis of hunger finding dry toast
In monsoon desert outside of Hollywood

Michael A. J. Sardo

Are You Undecided?

To buy a ring, car or house. Or picture frame
Or see a good friend. Or go to sleep, maybe
Waking up next week or never. To fall in or
Out of love. Caulking up the air seams
Of the inside walls of your home. A cardboard
Refrigerator box laying on the street: somewhere
To sleep. In your homeless environment.
To take a train, bus or plane to go to Scandia or
Cleveland, Ohio. Or to jump off the Brooklyn
Bridge, Williamsburg Bridge or the Merry-go-round
Don't be a decision maker now. Wait for a critique
And then blow the wad in your pocket? Now.
Don't see your psychoanalyst

Let's Just be Friends

The emotional pain was more than he could handle
Seemed like old times were ancient times
The statement blew what was left of his mind
After being two or more quarts low.
The words rang in his mind. A true story.
Without a story-line of faith, hope and charity
Friendship died up on the outskirts of a different lifestyle
Did Bauldelaire write about this in Les Fleurs du Mal?
Endless sweet raindrops touched the sensuous mouth
After being lovers once. Being friends had nothing to do with it.
It was his first time being dumped like a rag doll
Rejection! Rejection! Is that my surname?

Michael A. J. Sardo

A Small Brown Bag Please

Waiter! The remains to fill my hungry tummy
Waiter! The brown bag please
Waiter! At least a small brown bad filled with O's
The remains were always the same. Waiter!
Dog-eared paper colored brown. Dirty brown.
Truffles, cups of wine spilled over a tent
Comes Sunday no cup to fill not even
A small brown bag. Please. A corkscrew, a
Funnel, a cheese grater, could all fit in the
Small brown bag. Temperatures rise, wells
Dry up and no sight of the little brown bag
A courtroom filled with trash emptying
Out in the Dundel Forrest of leftovers

Cold Storage

Came a muted thump at my door. Minus 32 degrees
A marble slab on which to sleep. Grommet
Faced creature of the night. Don't pluck out his beard. Timeless
Catapult in the upper cloudless colony. Opal
Cadet a retiree. Bladina. A critical study
Once upon a time. Blue was the mode. Fashion
Surely wasn't the character. It's somewhere Keep
Looking. No worrying about the future.
Captain Kirk has a hangnail
Waiting to apply in the parallelism of Time
See you next week, after the expedition, Mr. Spock

Michael A. J. Sardo

The Tone Key was Frosted

A quick flick of the aching wrist
The muted transfer of feeling traveling cold up the arm
The opulence of titanium found very little
Time to enter the world of privation. The
Tone key made very little restitution in those days
Harboring ill feeling along the way. An antiquated way
The frosted Tone key, worked wonders on the blow-hard
Determined to strip his consciousness of all the deterrents
Of limbo. Opening his ego-centric vast wasteland,
Of dormant thoughts and emotions. Embracing
His past, present and future ongoing nightmares
Escaping in his anxious day-dreaming fantasies

Request Denied

By popular demand the answer was No
A positive assertion was not in sight anywhere
Finding the wrong spot was relatively easy
Glamorous women always in search of empty think tanks
A barking dog, a hissing cat created chaos in the street
A starving beggar crying out in the streets of Bombay
A disproportionate onslaught of hunger dominated the affluent neighborhood
Carriers of lead boxes. Downtrodden they seemed able
To blackout from hunger. It was even an effort
To vomit nothing. Just air spewed out. A
Penny would have given some relief in the marketplace
Always they walked away closing their ears and eyes
To the hurt of requests that were always denied.
Tried and proven were the multitude of calamities
No. Meant No! In any language of dark streets
Even in the affluent city streets.

Michael A. J. Sardo

Overextended and Nervous

A high roller taxed out to the max
Spending as much as he could get
Living in overextended prosperity
Anything she wanted she got
Tranquilized from an envelope in a glass of water
There was no second call. Just the
Rattle of aching bones and a wailing
Pocket calendar voice-activated by
The invisible man. Where was H.G. Wells,
Orson Wells, The Wolfman or Steven King
Somewhere in the desert of nervousness. The oasis
Combined with the pauper cemetery and friends

An Imperfection that Never Counted

-Looking with eyes alone-
The genetic superstructure collided with the traditional values
The slight slant around the eyes
The skin tone darkened. Not by the sun
The pure white skin and the features of a dark-skinned one.

All playing havoc on pre-judgmental thinking
A disturbance as destructive as Vesuvio
Or a hurricane ravaging the East Coast of the USA
Or a quake that killed thousands in India
                    -Looking with eyes alone-
            Their imperfections never counted
Because they became Famous Musicians
                Famous Lawyers
                Famous Authors
                Famous Surgeons
                Famous Historians
                Famous Opera Stars
                Famous Actors
                Famous Entrepreneurs
                Famous Diplomats
                Famous Clergymen
                Famous Scientists
                Famous Missionaries
                Famous Scholars
                Famous Poets
                Famous Novelists
                Famous Playwrites

Michael A. J. Sardo

Adversity and Youth

Striking one blow after another
Hoping, wishing, examining the downloads of adolescence
Point a finger at life's environmental displeasures
Missing the mark now and again
Dusting the hi-power rose petal powder in your nostrils
Throw away money, you don't have. But wished you had
Sitting on the analyst's couch. Playback your dreams
Somewhere in the span of preteen hood you die
A natural death of disappointment and rejection. Find
Me a clinic Mr. Freudian Doctor. Where exploding
Desires, emotions, find their way in the wax chamber
Of my head. Teenager you line up your desires
And descend on the whiskey bottle of unfulfilled
Dreams. Pressures, emotions and daytime nightmares

Fear of What

Being rejected and left out
Being accepted and being alone
Yourself without any inhibitions
Making a mistake you'll regret the rest of your life
Being loved and maybe for just a season
Being yourself and afraid of losing everyone
Of declaring your independence from the whole system
What they'll say when you've been exposed
Afraid of being exploited because of your talent
Consumed by a burning desire to make a statement
Trying something new and coming short of the mark
Authority you hate and being victimized in time and space
Indifference to your affections and pronouncements
Of leaving a meaningless legacy
Of hiding a past full of camouflaged emotions

Michael A. J. Sardo

Lovers in Love

Flowers, candy, perfumes. Fill the damp nights of the city
Some choose the outdoor treks
Others invade the private chambers of libraries
Looking and experiencing a newness never sensed before
The tingle of finger tips, touching, arousing with very little temperance
A delicate scent of flowers, yet to be named
Dominated by the gentle wind of the ocean breezes
Something within them both gives the two of
you a feeling of delectable fear
Not forboding, but almost forbidden
Letters of love laced with delicate perfumed tinctures
A chemistry of elements coming together never experienced before
A school with no formal curriculum
Students of all ages and varied backgrounds, contending gentle negotiations
Hovering over them and overwhelming spirit of refraction
With love conceding to none. The choice was made. For
Them, they didn't know how it happened nor cared
Enamored, smitten, enchanting. Lovers in love

Marriage Vows

Taken by some lightly. By others painfully commanding
Pulling out the stops on the way
All kinds of residual promissory notes
On paper, in blood and honor. Not one overbearing in essence
Never to be broken. From Japan to America
From freedom to tyranny. Usurping continents
Examples shared in tropical habitats. Or desert
Tents or smoky cities encouraging outcries of endearment
Considering the intellectual decision. Examine the marriage vows

Michael A. J. Sardo

Memory Never Failing

Recollections
Recalling
Remembrances
Calling to mind
Flashbacks
Of lucid
Childhood animations
And sane, rational
Unremembered trespasses
Reminiscent of lunatic parents
Living in a house of disorder
Frenzied by a ranting, raving
Mother of madness
Insane with jealousy of everyone
Adhering to no discretion
Understanding and intelligence
Being compressed in a corner of a small bedroom
Assenting to trusting doctrines of
Mistrust, suspicion and very little credulous worth
A slow fearful itinerant
Lacking navigational skills
Living in never failing honeycombs of
Transmitted memories in a never failing memory

A Multitude of Problems

Starting off with one's frightening concealments
Comes an onslaught of curious, flickering difficulties
Hit hard with the sledge hammer of despair
Failures knocking at the glass door of your heart
Disappointments find the parallel courses being scanned
Competition for some prize possession not needful ever
Well-wishes storming the bastions of your cottage
Rejection and cowardice timidly establishing strongholds
Lawsuits you didn't invite or approve of
Decays of matter and dominant obsessions
Fatigue arriving in the predestined time
Compromise mid-way across the field of illusions
Ancestral bi-focal qualifying hereditary actions seen
Plummeting down from the jetty sky
Hunger, sickness and disease in the third worlds

Michael A. J. Sardo

Without Music

A silence so dead robots can only hear
No such equivocal empathy voicing a rage of impatience
Even the human voice experiences mental excitation
No music. Just a tinitus sound emanation in a human head
The empty soundless vacuum of an incandescent lamp.
A Mozartian tragedy overlooked in the space of time
There would be no transfusion of sentiment
There stood a greenhouse of plant-less species
There would be no color to emblazon the mind.
Finding no whiteness in a colorless world
Finding no ebony to blot out the world of gray
Void of music there would be no understanding
Of silver, brown, red, green, yellow, purple
Blue and orange, discerning perceptions
Of yet to be explored galaxies in outer space

A Depressing Day

A refresher course you always wanted to take. And never did
Get yourself organized! Regroup. Avoid the day
Determine what volume of poetry you dare read
Blow everything out of proportion
Pop one pill after another
Rejection comes in different sudden flashes
Being wrong puts you in an addictive flash of thought
Evil drawbacks plead anguish and outrage. Aggression
Fear of losing love. An invention of cruel mental suffering
A cloudy cold dungeon of a day.
Picking up a dusty volume of a "Cycle of Poems in Experimentation"
A flashback of wicked women called mothers
Finding illegal contraband under your pillow
Pitfalls of being young and failing to leave a legacy
A vast undertaking you might not handle
Finally a visit to a psychiatric museum in the Midwest
Leaving the place behind and all its diversified artifacts
A pleasantly hospitable depressing day

Michael A. J. Sardo

Patience and Poverty

Said the rich man to the hungry man, just wait.
You'll find work for yourself and your children will be okay
Maybe that hungry man will turn to the rich man's philosophy
And be patient, while his family goes hungry.
Do all those people really need all that food the pantry gives out?
I'm sure there's plenty of work. Are they really poor? That poor
Said the rich man. Where can I go to buy cheap food too
Do they really appreciate what they're getting free?
So what if they wait for things to get better. Where's their patience?
Just wait. Poor people have to be patient. It might be the Lord's will
Time will just be patient a little bit more. The economy
Will pick up. I just lost a lot of money in the stock market
This country gives too much overseas
Thanks for listening to me.
A Church-going friend of the poor. Signed Mr. Generous

Time Waits for No One

Especially death when no one's around
Claiming victory after victory on time
Even a beautiful child is never kept waiting
As the curtain goes down. Time never says timeout
Longing to be alone in the compartments of the mind
The essence of the senses stop then and there
Redeem lost time. Impossible like a serpent's sting
The interval of the drama. Like unto an instantaneous intermission
Why waste when you can spend it luxuriously
No one is taken by surprise, not even the expendable ones
Even the drop of water forming into a vapor
No one is kept aloof. Mother, Father. No repose
Brother, Sister, Son or Daughter. Times up No other recourse
Even Time's absence remains in short endless durations
Hoot owl in a barn the clock struck twelve and
Nobody made a decision for you, except Father Time

Michael A. J. Sardo

Best Wishes

Are the dreams you never owned. Were they yours?
The slippery fingers that held tight to the Promised Land
Or the elephant walk you took through the black window
The promise of another Gung Ho! Disappointment.
A bear trap that almost cost your foot
The time you almost fell asleep driving on the Freeway
A subway car door, that opened on the wrong side
Remember looking down on the Third Rail on Essex Street
You almost walked off the elevator shaft 22 stories down
The bus didn't stop to pick you up. And they laughed at you
Compliments of the Well Wishers International
Who, are your good friends in waiting Now and then

Best Wishes. You're still alive

E. A. Poe a Genius

A nibbling vibrato. Coming from the black cat in the window
He had ravens and good friends. Who knew his mastery
Of words symbols and things. The pendulum swung
His pen stood out among the immortal writers
Poetic liberty was a featured greatness in E. A. Poe verses
His great talent gave birth to a hemisphere of dark innocence
He took his Annabel Lee to heights of greatness in his love
Helen of Troy was made jealous of this child
A fire in E. A. Poe's breast drew him to ecstatic
Excitement. Inevitably his persevering spirit made contact
A short four decades was his term of office
Ending in the gloom and shadow of a monkey's paw

Michael A. J. Sardo

Instant Gluttony

A spoonful of grease
Two measures of sugar
Settling somewhere in the gut
Swallow up belly-bomber
Intoxicated with fried stuff
Harsh hot sauces
Plenty of cream dressings
The wrath of hot salsa
Lost rudiments of nutrition
White flour paste
Out of date coffee mud
Frigidaire full of nothing
Sour upsurge tempered by lemon drops
County Fair funnel cake
A dead end spew
Ethnic food bar internationale
Start with over-the-counter fire retardants
Back up of acid reflux
Something stronger to take
Overload! Overload!
Three days of living dangerously
Try again instant gluttony
No way out
STOP! Eating at Lucy Martinez' house

Disagreement Comes in Different Colors

Fabricated emotional impromptus flavored with resentment
Coordinated with unruly affections, two-thirds of the way
Dominated by incoherent humorless impressions
The physical disagreement is not the color issue
Issues plague suffering modern day saints. Where's
Leon's hopefulness. On the other side of the paranoia syndrome
Or is it in the skeleton of a closed casket. Trust no one
And prepare for another lugubrious affair. Build a
Castle full of false humility and an outcome of nothing.
Disagree with no one disburse all kinds of ironic congratulations
Promise no passionate social interaction. Differences
Come together in different color packages or disagreement

Michael A. J. Sardo

A Bottle of Coke

Jump in the dirty old pond
The money you saved wasn't worth it
Endless underwater creatures make the coke bottle slippery
A 95 degree-in-the-shade bottle of coke quenches the internal fire
Product lines disappear like unexpected breezes
A bottle of coke would taste good in the catacombs
Or in the mummy's tomb. Or Count Alacard's Castle
A bottle of coke would taste good on Academy Award's night,
Or in Bates Motel, or in the Globe Theatre during intermission
A bottle of coke. I'd give my life for a bottle of coke
Even on a Pirate Ship on the Spanish Main. No bottle of coke

Adventurous Angela

Crying out for adventurous love and there was none
Find affection from some old guy, old enough to be your-
And there was no affection anywhere
Be a dreamer lonely, lonely Angela
Adventurous Angela too smart to get hurt
To pretty to be snobbish Miss Angela
A touch of class. Desirable to the intellectual few
Times up. There's no clowns or dummies around
Angela have you ever launched a ship!
Or read about the well of emptiness

Michael A. J. Sardo

There is No Boundary Line

Or comfort zone, or pressure relief zone
Not even a boundary line to call your own
The death rattle makes no plays for time
Where is the boundary line? Between Heaven and Hell
Between truth and fiction, between positive and negative
Between time and space, Bow and Arrow
There is no boundary between poverty and starvation
Destruction and reparation, bolt and nut
Mind and brain, tombstone and crematorium
Boundary lines are made by uninformed ignorant souls who can't measure
Pleasure seekers, plunderers and soldiers of fortune
House cats and savage cats being endangered
Between fallen rock and landslides, volcano and earthquakes
Look for an atomic clock to find the time of day in the boundary line
There is no boundary line between insanity and genius
There is no boundary line
                    FINIS

Fortunate Unfortunates

In the wooded edge of the acreage past five points
Buried in the dirt cover with aged rocks and bones
Not hidden treasure, or a box of diamonds stolen
Lay the testament heart of a 20th century tragedy
Could have been Romeo and Juliet or Love Story
Neither one or the other. But Connie's work
She feverishly double-spaced the document
A hope of making it in publisher avenue
Or call it publisher's row. Unsympathetic editors
Fifty years went by and the old man's heart was gone
And the memory of a first novel which never made it
The manuscript of the Fortunate Unfortunates died with the author
Fifty years ago in time relegated space. Yesterday

Michael A. J. Sardo

Prescription Found

Easing pain and possible suffering
After the search for the higher ground
There was a backside of illegal street trafficker
Where all kinds of prescription easements were filled
No need for the medical document. The gentleman
With all the reptilian tattoos lived on illegal street
The smoke-filled rooms of Illegal Street
Used by the unlicensed distributors of medicinal canals
Make-believe dispensed for sociological paralyzers
Never free because the socialization was governed
By the political representatives and all the free-
Thinkers and Left-wingers almost the wrong
Slip of paper. Then legislation was passed
And the prescription was found at last. A forgery

Learning Never Ends

Although according to the standards of the purveyors
Of the intelligentsia crowds never gathered to
Help the brilliant one suffering from inferiority
He tried to intellectualize. Gave the appearance of dementia
His hidden secret in his sculpt management face
Even in the presence of criticism his writing prevailed
Studying every writer the bookseller could furnish
Year after year his understanding of the truth grew
Listening, reading, seeing, appreciating finally was his
End. Dying with questions in his mouth. He never stopped
Inquiring. He was misunderstood in his lifetime of quest

Michael A. J. Sardo

Hearing is Believing

Winching is grieving. As though sounds lived
Listening to the string section. In time of elation
Voices from a far off signaling help is near
The cheering crowd at that Gladiator. Thumbs
Down. The riot noise at the Guillotine in Paris
The screams of souls, torments of Hell
Starving poor in streets, moaning from hunger
Crying children, lonely, hungry for something to eat
The Satanic noise from the evil crowd at public lynchings
A crackling fire and screams of death. Before the fire
Trucks arrive, the marching band, cheering the team
Drops of water from a leaking faucet. Eating at your nerves
A screaming, ranting, spoiled mother destroying her young child's mind
Ocean sounds minding the seaweed smell
Dropping a tray of food causing silence to prevail in the cafeteria
Foghorns of neighboring Tugs. Announcing sinisterism
Clapping blades of chopper flying overhead
Explosions, one after another in the Viet Cong camp
The wailing of a Banshee on celluloid to be viewed
Organ pipes fill the Cathedral of light in music
The audio device causing faith and hope

No Way Out

You pulled the trigger, the premeditated act. Fulfilled
The child abuser succumbed to the power urge. Caught
One lie after another, the act-perpetrated. Perjury
The taking of a life, the endless loop video. On and on
You adjusted the corporate books. In your favor. In jail now
Play a game, loving another's wife and got caught. Divorce
Play the same game, not so nice husband: bullet in head
Addicted to popping pills, drinking gin. Headaches
Impulsive pronouncement refusing amends. A loss
Action motivated by imprudent actions dominating mobiles
Shadow of illusion obliteration of a memory. Amnesia
Visionary look at life, through rose-colored glasses

Michael A. J. Sardo

The Time of Inequality is Over

Time marched on, down Southern Times Counties
Look now!
Black Judges, black Doctors, black Teachers, black Politicians
Times up. It's all over
European immigrant from all over taking their
Rightful place. Earned, not given
Born. The new policy. USA 21st Century
Hispanic Lawyers, Hispanic Churches, in the melting
Pot of the big city. Newcomers making their way
Asian Musicians, Mathematicians, Composers, Scientists
Traveling the timeless hall of fame
The disfigured, the impaired, the lame, the disoriented,
In wheelchairs, white canes, with dogs and walkers
The time of inequality is over. Finally.

2001 Now What Utopia

The green lush grass underfoot. Breathes clean air.
Unpolluted streams, rivers, lakes and oceans
All endangered species, no longer endangered
No more Titan smoke stack belching toxic gases
Never more the pain and struggle for intellect
An end to the plagues, diseases and pain
Interplanetary exchange of ideas. No thought of differences
The essence of internal turmoil eradicated, once and for all
Documented advances in human civilization recorded,
Planetary concord relations completed. In the galaxy.
Anger, pain, jealousy, hatred, prejudice isolated. Slate
Clean. When all is said and done. Look for
2001. As your best year of existence.
Relinquish the broadband dynamo of Time-travel
It's not heaven yet. Not the perfections imagined
This all was recorded in a time capsule called
Utopia 2001. Now what?

Michael A. J. Sardo

Prelude to Hate

Astounded by so powerful an emotion
How could there be so much insubordination
Even among the ascetics
Programming the unlawful mind
A fallen sparrow shot by child with a BB gun
Or the insensitive mother wanting attention
While her child lay dying in a hospital bed
Pious one being put down while studying Alcoran
A child being beaten by a hostile parent for being a child
Falcon's chicks being harassed by investigators
Find it impossible to be kind and understanding
Discovering sexuality in innocence, receiving
Punishment by a mother enjoying the pleasure of
Inflicting pain and torment
Who is she, this polar witch of the city
And laughing while causing mental convulsive dolor
Can't see the handwriting on the fogged mirror

Actions Speak Louder than Good Intentions

In a small town, and observation
Thinking of helping that poor family down the street
By bringing a food basket. Simply forgot, garden club
Auction, shopping in that new Mall
Thinking of helping out in the soup kitchen
O shucks, I didn't remember, got myself on my mind.
Can't they find work? There's work for retarded people
Do they have to beg all the time? They need their own kind
It would be nice if someone would visit that nursing home
Smells like a zoo in there. I'm too nervous
Bring that old stuff that you were going to throw away
They're poor, they'll take anything
Getting up so early in the morning to help the kids,
Go to free Kids Camp. Let the city people help
You said this and not that. Dire circumstances
Every intension disclosed found some passive excuse
Just a certain observation in a small town

Michael A. J. Sardo

Circus in Your Mind

Clamorous sounding heartbeats
Electronic sound vibrations from time to time
Then a speechless silence
Echoing carousel music shuttling from ear to brain
Rhythm hard to modulate
Common sense ticket takers
Symmetrical discordant euphonic melodies
Grab the brass ring, find out it was nothing
Wild animals, clowns, barker and bearded ladies,
The midget people in a world of their own
Freaks to world. And then there was the Elephant Man

The Evil Eye

The child was nervous as a child could be
Enough being a change of life baby
He got sick as any child would get sick
White-haired mother, high-strung, selfish
The boy was given the Evil Eye. A widow lady
Then a spaghetti dish filled with water
Candles burning, she uttered incantations
Evil Spirits. There were none in the child.
Mother white-haired was probably one herself
Then a spritzing of olive oil in the watered
Dish. The eyes would come out. Evil Eyes
At the sign of no relief. A purgative was
Administered rectally. Gone was the Evil
Eye. And then the old Sicilian lady felt relief
In those days doctors made house calls

9 780595 195848